Taming Babel

By Anna Wing-bo Tso

Illustrated by Joanne Lo

Dedication

From Anna Wing-bo Tso : To all 73.3 million native speakers of Cantonese, as well as anyone who loves Cantonese.

From Joanne : To my cousin Ryan Ng, Caroline Wong, Vincent Chen, Julian Wong, Antina Lieu and my nephew Wesley Austin Wong.
To my friends too, who enjoy citing the classic quotes from Stephen Chow's movies all the time - Kay, Ambrielle, Hester and Dave.

Acknowledgements

We would like to take this opportunity to express our immense gratitude to our muses - Arisa, Evelyn, and Carmen. We are also greatly indebted to Professor Taciana Fisac of the Autonomous University of Madrid, who gave us her professional suggestions and wrote the inspiring foreword for us. Last but not least, we are grateful to the Sunrise Charitable and Education Fund, which sponsored the publication of our *Hong Kong Stories* series (reference no.: S/V/EL in U001 (8/2016)).

Foreword

Imagine all the flowers around the world having the very same colour. Or imagine just a few varieties of trees were growing in the forests of each continent and there were only a few species of animals. Different types of flowers, trees and animals make nature much more interesting. Diversity is a very special aspect because it enriches our planet, and in a similar way, languages and cultures are a unique expression of the experience of people in different places.

When we are little we learn to use a certain language, and that language helps us express our emotions. Being able to speak and write in Cantonese is as significant as learning and using any other language. All the languages spoken around the world are unique, important and interesting. And this story will help you to understand how fun and rich it can be to speak Cantonese, your mother tongue or your friends' mother tongue. Let's talk in Cantonese!

Taciana Fisac, PhD
Professor of Chinese Literature &
Founding Director of the Centre of Studies of Eastern Asia
Autonomous University of Madrid

Linguists have been telling us English is the world's franca lingua, but sometimes, if a language is fun and beautiful enough, people may just as well employ it and forget about using English all the time.

Case One

A Japanese speaking Cantonese

Case One: A Japanese Speaking Cantonese

Arisa, my Japanese student, once shared in the linguistics class that Cantonese vocabulary is easier than many foreigners may have imagined.

Who doesn't know loan words such as **Tofu** (bean curd), **Peking duck** (roast duck), **Chow Mein** (stir-fried noodles), and **Kung Fu** (martial arts) ?

Tofu

Peking duck

Chow Mein

Dim Sum

" Just like Katakana in Japanese, loan words borrowed from English have fully integrated into Cantonese too. Learn the loan words and you will be able to communicate in Cantonese with Hong Kong people easily. "She then proudly showed us the Chinese flash cards (with standard Cantonese pronunciation) she used to learn Cantonese, which totally touched and surprised all Hong Kong classmates:

班戟
baan¹ kik¹
PANCAKE

多士
dor¹ si²
TOAST

忌廉
gei⁴ lim¹
CREAM

奄列
am¹ lit⁶
OMELETTE

Case Two: A Filipino Speaking Cantonese

My Filipino friend, Evelyn is also a fan of Cantonese. She can speak fluent English, but having worked as a domestic helper for a Hong Kong family for more than thirty years, she prefers speaking Cantonese with us in Hong Kong. Curious about the way she learnt Cantonese, a language entirely different from her mother tongue, I asked Evelyn how she started to learn Cantonese.

To my astonishment, Evelyn has developed a systematic way of building her Cantonese vocabulary, and she is still building it. She explained, "Many Cantonese expressions sound very similar to English ones. Even though I do not know how to write or read Chinese characters, I can memorize Cantonese terms well quite easily." The following is an excerpt from Evelyn's notes:

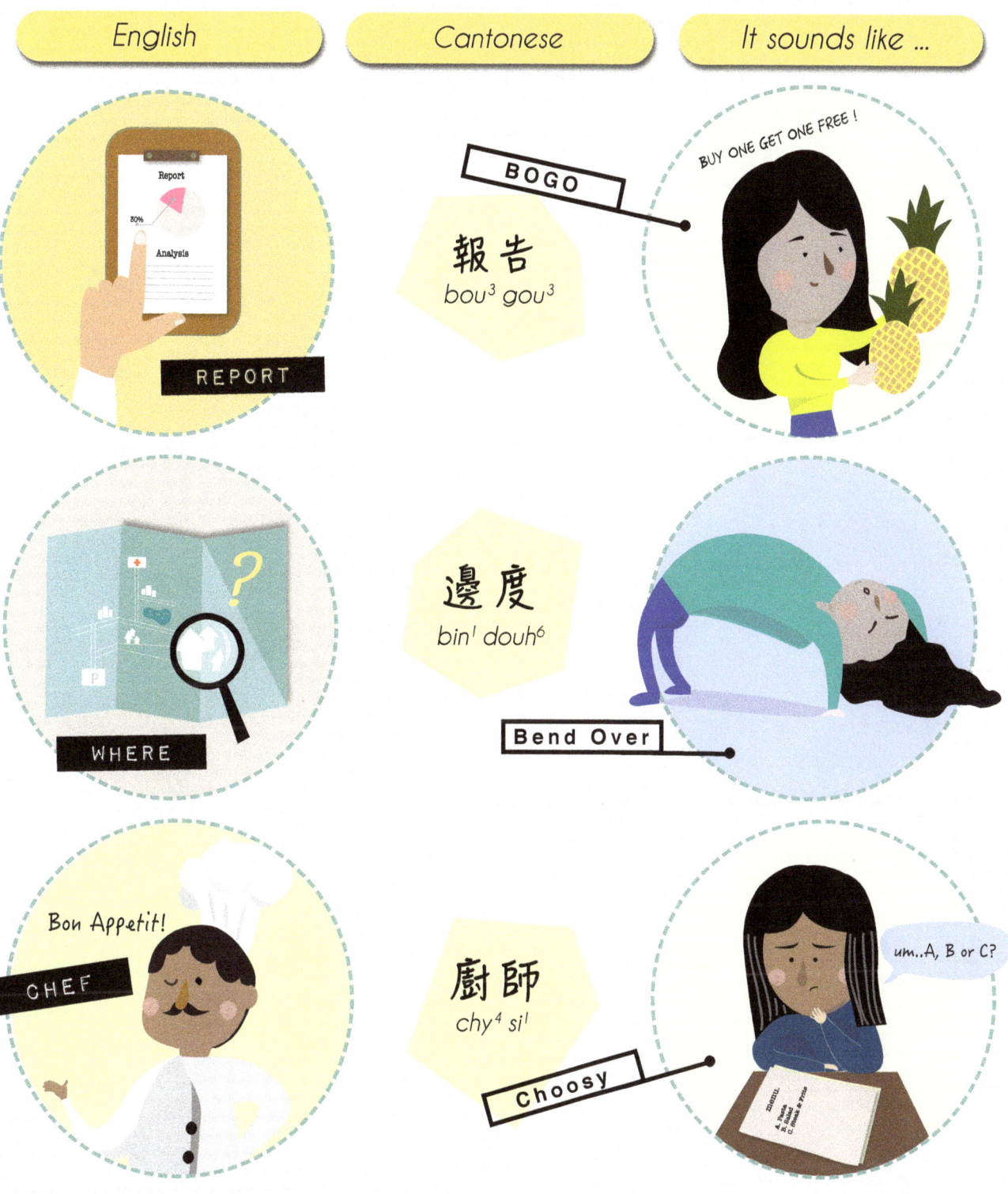

Case Three

A Canadian speaking Cantonese

Case Three: A Canadian Speaking Cantonese

Arisa and Evelyn are not the only foreigners who love to use Cantonese in Hong Kong. My ex-colleague, Carmen is yet another Cantonese lover. Carmen is a native English teacher from Canada. She has been working for a secondary school in Hong Kong for more than ten years now.

She revealed that her love for Cantonese began with watching Hong Kong superstar Stephen Chow's comedy movies, in which she realized Cantonese sounds and tones are as beautiful as a musical scale, but can be extremely difficult to learn:

「余與汝，遇於雨。
yú yǔ rǔ, yù yú yǔ

汝語余，於雨餘。
rǔ yù yú, yú yǔ yú

於汝寓，汝娛余。」
yú rǔ yù, rǔ yú yú

黃霑撰

You and I, met in the rain.

While it was still raining, you said to me,

"Come to my place. I'll bring you comfort."

— By James Wong

Speaking the language is like singing son
according to Carm

Most challenging of all, the slightest variation in sound and tone can change the lexical meaning of a Cantonese word completely. Here are but a few examples Carmen mentioned to me:

Cantonese

女友 / 旅遊

nui⁵ yauh⁵   lui⁵ yauh⁴

GIRLFRIEND   # TRAVEL

Cantonese

着衫 / 初三

chueh³ saam¹   cho¹ saam¹

PUT ON ONE'S CLOTHES

THIRD DAY OF CHINESE NEW YEAR

Cantonese

等我太太 / 等我睇睇

dang² ngo⁵ tai² tai² / dang² ngo⁵ taai³ taai³*²

\# WAIT FOR MY WIFE   \# LET ME TAKE A LOOK

Cantonese

正 / 靜

zing³   zing⁶

\# SUPERB   \# QUIET

As a language teacher, Carmen wants to prove to her students that a language as hard as Cantonese can be learned well through hard work. She is also convinced that if she can conquer Cantonese, she will be able to master any language with ease.

> As a native Cantonese speaker in Hong Kong, I feel really proud and thankful.

Book series author

Anna Wing-bo Tso is an associate professor of English and Comparative Literature at The Open University of Hong Kong. Interested in children's literature, gender studies, language arts and translation studies, Anna has organized numerous international conferences in her areas of expertise and published research articles in peer-reviewed journals across Asia, Europe, the U.K., the U.S., Canada, Australia and New Zealand. She is the author of the *Hong Kong Stories* series (Alpha Academic Press, 2017 -), the first author of *Academic Writing for Arts and Humanities Students* (McGraw-Hill, 2016), the co-author of *Teaching Shakespeare to ESL Students* (Springer, 2017), and the associate editor of Springer's *Digital Culture and Humanities* book series. In her free time, she also writes and publishes plays, poems, short stories, and children's picture books for leisure. Her prose and verse have appeared in literary periodicals and national newspapers, including *The Font, American Tanka, New Academia, and China Times*.

Book series illustrator

Joanne Lo was born in Canada and raised both in Toronto and Hong Kong. Having grown up and living on a beautiful outlying island called Cheung Chau, she has a special love for nature, animals, art and one's spiritual growth. She began her career in creative media since graduating from university majoring in Cultural Studies and Visual Studies. She is the illustrator of *Teaching Shakespeare to ESL Students* (Springer, 2017), a book housed in the Yale and Harvard University Libraries and downloaded for over 10,630 times since its publication.

Hong Kong Stories
The Complete Series

Tailor-made for young readers at ages 8 - 12 in Hong Kong and beyond, the *Hong Kong Stories* series is a collection of English stories written with the local Hong Kong context in mind. Ideal for language learning, leisure and reading aloud among readers young and old, the book series brings together original short stories and pictures about various aspects of Hong Kong's everyday life:

Book 1: *Culinary Charades*, a taster of Hong Kong food
Book 2: *The Summer of 1997*, a walk down memory lane in Hong Kong
Book 3: *Unforgettable Neighbours*, a Hong Kong animal safari
Book 4: *Taming Babel*, the serendipity of the Cantonese language
Book 5: *Herstory*, a tribute to Hong Kong women
Book 6: *A Tale of Two Haunted Universities*, a spooky Halloween treat

www.ingramcontent.com/pod-product-compliance
Lightning Source LLC
Chambersburg PA
CBHW041215240426
43661CB00012B/1049